THE UNFORGIVING SERVANT

MATTHEW 18

"I got it," laughed Todd as he caught the yellow Frisbee and threw it back.

"Good throw, little brother!" exclaimed Leo as he whisked the Frisbee back to Todd. Back and forth the Frisbee went. Todd was happy to spend time with his brother, and he didn't want the fun to end.

"Do you want to play something else, Leo?" asked Todd. "Maybe with that nice new remote control helicopter you just got?

“I wish I could,” replied Leo as he stopped to catch his breath. “I have to meet up with some friends.”

“Well, can I play with it?” asked Todd.

“It’s not easy to fly,” replied Leo as he went to the gate. “Wait till I get back and we can play together. OK?”

Todd watched sadly as his brother left. Since he couldn't think of anything else to do, he tried playing with the Frisbee by himself, but that didn’t last long. Next, he played on the swing, then kicked the ball, finally deciding to go inside and watch a DVD.

Passing by the open door of his brother's room, he saw the shiny new helicopter.

"Oh boy!" he exclaimed, and then he went in.

At first, all Todd wanted to do was look at the toy, at how nice it was and how great the colors looked.

"Wow!" he thought out loud. "I wonder what it would be like to fly it."

Soon the sounds of the flying helicopter filled the room. Todd was happily flying the toy and having a great time, when.... "I'm home!" Leo had just walked through the downstairs door.

Afraid that Leo would catch him playing with his new toy, Todd hurriedly tried to land it, but in his haste, he moved the controls too quickly. Suddenly, there was the sound of a crash. Todd's eyes widened.

“Hi, Todd!” Leo said, as he walked up the stairs.

Todd didn’t even look at his brother, but instead quickly made his way down the stairs and to the door. No sooner had his hand touched the doorknob than he heard his brother yell from upstairs: “TODD!”

“Oh, no!” thought Todd to himself, as he slowly turned back to the stairs.

Todd walked into his brother's room and saw the helicopter, bent and broken, in his brother's hands.

"I told you to wait till I got back," Leo said firmly and sadly. "Now look at my helicopter!"

Todd felt very, very bad and could think of nothing to say. "I'm sorry!" he cried. He knew that saying sorry would not fix the broken toy, so he cried even louder.

Seeing his younger brother cry made Leo feel bad for him. “It’s ok, Todd,” he said.

“What? Really?” Todd asked as he wiped away his tears.

“Yes, really,” Leo sighed. “Maybe I can fix it. I forgive you.”

“Oh, Leo! You’re the best!” said Todd happily. “And I am really, really sorry I didn't listen to you.” Just then, the doorbell rang. Todd heard his mother call him downstairs, because his friends had come over.

Todd ran into the back yard, just as his friend Charlie picked up his yellow Frisbee. “Let’s play with this!” Charlie exclaimed, as he threw the Frisbee. Up into the air it soared, and then… it landed right in a very tall tree, out of reach.

Todd was very upset. “Look at what you did! That was my favorite Frisbee, and now it’s stuck up in that tree!”

“I’m really sorry,” cried Charlie. “I didn’t mean to.”
But Todd would not listen to his friend. “I’m not going to play with you anymore!” he yelled. Right as he said that, Leo’s helicopter flew out the window into plain view.

At first, Todd was surprised to see it. It looked like Leo had done a fine job of fixing it. Then, he noticed that the helicopter was carrying something. It was carrying "The Jesus Stories!"

"Jesus stories, Jesus stories!
Is there a Jesus story in the book for me!
Jesus stories, Heaven's glories!
Just open up the book and you can see!"

"I think there is something in the book that might help," said Leo as he opened the book and began to read.

Once upon a time, there was a king that had a servant who owed him a lot of money. The servant didn't have the money and so he could not pay the king back.

"Please, sire!" begged the servant. "I just can't pay back this money! I have tried, but I don't have enough to pay you!"

Seeing the poor man cry, the king felt sorry for him. "Alright. Don't cry. You do not have to pay me back. I will forgive your debt."

Well, the servant was so happy! He danced his way out of the castle, laughing for joy. He was so very thankful.

Suddenly, he saw a man he knew. “You!” said the servant who was no longer smiling. Grabbing the man by the coat, he said, “You owe me some money and you have not paid it back!”

“But… I… I just don’t have the money! I tried to pay you but I don’t have enough! Can you give me more time or forgive me?” cried the poor man.

“Forgive you?” yelled the servant. “I will not forgive you! You will pay me back what you owe me right now, or I will take you to jail!”

The news of the way his servant had treated the poor man came to the ears of the king. Soon, the servant found himself in the king's throne room.

"I forgave you for not paying me back. I felt sorry for you because you could not," said the king. "This man owes you much less than you owe me, and yet you treated him very badly. You said you would not forgive him. You said he was going to jail."

The servant was very scared. "Well, I..." he blurted out, but the king stopped him.

“Take this bad servant away!” said the king to his guards. “And make sure he pays me back everything he owes.” Then, facing the servant as he was being taken away, the king added: “You should have treated others kindly, in the same way I treated you!”

As the story ended, Todd was very quiet.

"I'm sorry I was so mean to you, Charlie," he said. "Leo forgave me for much worse. I forgive you for losing my Frisbee. Will you forgive me for getting angry with you and for not forgiving you?"

"Of course I will," said Charlie happily, as Leo looked on smiling. Just then, the Frisbee floated down from the tree. "Look!" said Margie. "Mr. Wiggles pushed the Frisbee down! Your Frisbee isn't lost after all!"

"Then what are we waiting for?" said Todd. Soon they were all happily playing together.

In the same way that God forgives our sins and has mercy on us, He expects us to forgive and have mercy on others.